Betty Crocker

chocolate
treats

WILEY

Wiley Publishing, Inc.

D1512037

General Mills

Publishing Manager: Christine Gray

Editor: Grace Wells

Recipe Development and Testing:
Betty Crocker Kitchens

Photography and Food Styling: General
Mills Photography Studios and Image
Library

Wiley Publishing, Inc.

Publisher: Natalie Chapman

Associate Publisher: Jessica Goodman

Executive Editor: Anne Ficklen

Editor: Meaghan McDonnell

Production Manager: Michael Olivo

Production Editor: Abby Saul

Cover Design: Suzanne Sunwoo

Art Director: Tai Blanche

Layout: Indianapolis Composition
Services

Manufacturing Manager: Kevin Watt

This book is printed on acid-free paper. ⊛

For general information on our other products and services or for
technical support, please contact our Customer Care Department
within the United States at (877) 762-2974, outside the United States
at (317) 572-3993 or fax (317) 572-4002.

Wiley also publishes its books in a variety of electronic formats. Some
content that appears in print may not be available in electronic books.
For more information about Wiley products, visit our web site at www.
wiley.com.

Library of Congress Cataloging-in-Publication data is available upon
request.

ISBN: 978-0-470-87943-6

Manufactured in the United States of America

10 9 8 7 6 5 4 3 2 1

Our Betty Crocker Kitchens seal guar-
antees success in your kitchen. Every
recipe has been tested in America's
Most Trusted Kitchens™ to meet
our high standards of reliability, easy
preparation and great taste.

Find more great ideas at
BettyCrocker.com

Cover photo: Luscious Chocolate
Truffles (page 78)

Dear Friends,

Can't get enough chocolate? With this great collection of recipes, you can enjoy chocolaty cookies, decadent desserts and scrumptious bites with family and friends any time!

Who can resist freshly baked cookies and bars, especially with chocolate? Treat yourself with classic recipes like Extraordinary Chocolate Chip Cookies and Chocolate Brownies and new favorites like Cookies 'n Creme Brownies.

Nothing showcases chocolate quite like a decadent dessert! And don't worry—even when pressed for time, you can indulge in delicious cakes and tortes! Turn to the "Mix-it-Up with Chocolate" chapter, in which all the recipes, including Black Forest Cake and Triple-Chocolate Torte, use cake mixes. And if time allows, don't hesitate to take up the challenge of from-scratch recipes like Chocolate Cake with Raspberry Sauce and Chocolate Dream Tart.

Chocolate is equally delicious in bite-size treats, like Luscious Chocolate Truffles and Minty Fudge Cups. Or delight in rich Dark Chocolate Fondue or Chocolate Mousse. There can never be enough ways to treat yourself to chocolate!

Warmly,

Betty Crocker

chocolate treats

contents

chocolate basics

Cocoa beans are shelled, roasted and ground to make a thick paste called chocolate liquor, and cocoa butter is the fat or oil from the cocoa bean. Chocolate liquor is processed to make:

Semisweet, Bittersweet, Sweet and Milk Chocolate: Contain from 10 to 35 percent chocolate liquor, varying amounts of cocoa butter, sugar and, for some, milk and flavorings. Available in bars and chips for baking or eating.

Unsweetened Baking Cocoa: Dried chocolate liquor, with the cocoa butter removed, is ground into unsweetened cocoa. Cocoa drink mixes contain milk powder and sugar and are not a direct substitution for baking cocoa.

Unsweetened Chocolate: Contains 50 to 58 percent cocoa butter. Bitter in flavor, it's used primarily in baking.

"White" Chocolate: Is not true chocolate because it doesn't contain chocolate liquor. Made from cocoa butter, sugar, milk solids and vanilla. Often called white baking chips or vanilla baking bar.

melting chocolate

Melting chocolate isn't as easy as it may seem. It can become thick and grainy, and you may not have a clue what went wrong.

Melting Chocolate on the Stovetop

- Be sure the pan and utensils are dry because even a drop or two of water can cause chocolate to become stiff and grainy, which is known as "seizing."

- Use a heavy pan on very low heat and stir frequently to avoid scorching or burning the chocolate. Heat that's too high will also cause the chocolate to seize.

- Chopping the chocolate before melting helps the chocolate melt quicker.

- Stir the chocolate occasionally to prevent scorching. Also, by blending the solid pieces with the melted chocolate, the pieces will melt faster.

Correcting Seized Chocolate

If the smallest amount of moisture, such as steam, condensation or a few drops of water, comes in contact with chocolate while it melts, the chocolate will "seize," or turn grainy and hard. If this happens, remove the pan from the heat. With a whisk, stir in a liquid (warm water or milk, melted butter or margarine, vegetable oil or shortening), 1 tablespoon at a time, until the chocolate is smooth.

Seized chocolate is thick, dull and grainy.

Stir in a small amount of warm water until smooth and shiny.

Melting Chocolate in the Microwave

Baking Chocolate: Place 1 to 3 ounces unwrapped squares in a microwavable glass dish or measuring cup. Microwave uncovered on Medium 1½ to 1½ minutes, stirring frequently, until melted.

Chocolate Chips: Place ½ to 1 cup chips in microwavable glass bowl or glass measuring cup. Microwave uncovered on Medium 2 to 3 minutes, stirring frequently because chips will not change shape until melted.

cake basics

These basic tips for baking, storing and freezing cakes will be a great reference when you prepare the delicious cake recipes in this book.

Baking Cakes

- Place oven rack in the middle position.

- Place pans on the center of the rack. Arrange round cake pans so they don't touch, leaving at least one inch of space between pans and sides of the oven. When making a recipe that uses three round pans, refrigerate batter in third pan if all pans will not fit in the oven at one time; bake third pan separately.

- Spray pans with cooking spray or baking spray, or grease and flour pans as recommended in each recipe.

- Cool cakes that will not be removed from the pan, like 13 × 9-inch cakes, in the pan on a wire rack until completely cool. Cool cakes that will be removed from the pan, like round, fluted or tube pan cakes, in their pan(s) on wire racks for 5 to 10 minutes, then remove the cake and cool completely on cooling racks.

Storing Cakes

To store unfrosted cakes, cool cakes completely, at least one hour, before storing. If covered when warm, they become sticky and difficult to frost. Store loosely covered so the surface stays dry. Store cakes frosted with a creamy-type frosting under a cake safe (or large inverted bowl), or cover loosely with foil, plastic wrap or waxed paper. Store cakes frosted with whipped cream toppings or cream fillings in the refrigerator. Whether frosted or unfrosted, cakes with very moist ingredients, like applesauce, shredded carrots and mashed bananas, should be refrigerated during humid weather or in humid climates. If stored at room temperature, mold can grow quickly.

Freezing Cakes

To freeze unfrosted cakes, cool cakes completely, at least 1 hour. Place cakes in cardboard bakery boxes to prevent crushing, then cover with foil, plastic wrap or large food-storage freezer bags. Properly packaged, unfrosted cakes can be kept frozen 3 to 4 months. Frosted and glazed cakes freeze well, but the frosting or glaze may stick to the wrapping. To prevent sticking, freeze cake uncovered 1 hour, then insert toothpicks around the top and side of cake, and wrap. Frozen frosted cakes keep 2 to 3 months. Freeze cakes in single pieces or smaller portions to thaw quickly. Decorating gel, hard candies and colored sugars do not freeze well because they tend to run during thawing. It's best to decorate after cake is thawed.

cookies and bars

Chocolate Drop Cookies About 36 cookies

Prep Time: **25 Minutes**   Start to Finish: **1 Hour 25 Minutes**

COOKIES

1 cup granulated sugar

½ cup butter or margarine, softened

⅓ cup buttermilk

1 teaspoon vanilla

1 egg

2 oz unsweetened baking chocolate, melted, cooled

1¾ cups all-purpose flour*

½ teaspoon baking soda

½ teaspoon salt

1 cup chopped nuts, toasted if desired

CHOCOLATE FROSTING

2 oz unsweetened baking chocolate

2 tablespoons butter or margarine

2 cups powdered sugar

3 tablespoons hot water

1   Heat oven to 400°F. Grease cookie sheet with shortening or cooking spray, or line with cooking parchment paper or silicone baking mat.

2   In large bowl, beat granulated sugar, ½ cup butter, the buttermilk, vanilla, egg and melted chocolate with electric mixer on medium speed, or mix with spoon. Stir in flour, baking soda and salt. Stir in nuts.

3   On cookie sheet, drop dough by rounded tablespoonfuls about 2 inches apart.

4   Bake 8 to 10 minutes or until almost no indentation remains when touched in center. Immediately remove from cookie sheet to cooling rack. Cool completely, about 30 minutes.

5   In 2-quart saucepan, melt 2 oz chocolate and 2 tablespoons butter over low heat, stirring occasionally; remove from heat. Stir in powdered sugar and hot water until smooth. (If frosting is too thick, add more water, 1 teaspoon at a time. If frosting is too thin, add more powdered sugar, 1 tablespoon at a time.) Frost cookies.

*If using self-rising flour, omit baking soda and salt.

1 Cookie: Calories 150 (Calories from Fat 70); Total Fat 7g (Saturated Fat 3g); Cholesterol 15mg; Sodium 75mg; Total Carbohydrate 18g (Dietary Fiber 0g); Protein 2g

Extraordinary Chocolate Chip Cookies { About 6 dozen cookies }

Prep Time: **1 Hour**   Start to Finish: **1 Hour**

1½ cups butter or margarine, softened

1¼ cups granulated sugar

1½ cups packed brown sugar

1 tablespoon vanilla

2 eggs

4 cups all-purpose flour

2 teaspoons baking soda

½ teaspoon salt

1 bag (24 oz) semisweet chocolate chips (4 cups)

1   Heat oven to 350°F. In large bowl, beat butter, granulated sugar, brown sugar, vanilla and eggs with electric mixer on medium speed, or mix with spoon, until light and fluffy. Stir in flour, baking soda and salt (dough will be stiff). Stir in chocolate chips.

2   On ungreased cookie sheet, drop dough by tablespoonfuls 2 inches apart; flatten slightly.

3   Bake 11 to 13 minutes or until light brown (centers will be soft). Cool 1 to 2 minutes; remove from cookie sheet to cooling rack.

1 Cookie: Calories 140 (Calories from Fat 60); Total Fat 7g (Saturated Fat 4g); Cholesterol 15mg; Sodium 80mg; Total Carbohydrate 18g (Dietary Fiber 0g); Protein 1g

{ Making these cookies will go a lot faster if you use a cookie/ice-cream scoop. Level off the cookie dough in the scoop on the edge of the bowl. }

Double-Chocolate Cherry Cookies | About 4 dozen cookies

Prep Time: **1 Hour**   Start to Finish: **1 Hour**

1¼ cups sugar

1 cup butter or margarine, softened

¼ cup milk

¼ teaspoon almond extract

1 egg

1¾ cups all-purpose fl our

⅓ cup unsweetened baking cocoa

½ teaspoon baking soda

1 cup quick-cooking oats

1 cup semisweet chocolate chips

1 cup dried cherries

1 Heat oven to 350°F. In large bowl, beat sugar, butter, milk, almond extract and egg with electric mixer on medium speed until smooth. Stir in remaining ingredients.

2 On ungreased cookie sheet, drop dough by rounded tablespoonfuls about 2 inches apart.

3 Bake 10 to 12 minutes or until almost no indentation remains when touched in center and surface is no longer shiny. Immediately remove from cookie sheet to cooling rack.

1 Cookie: Calories 110 (Calories from Fat 45); Total Fat 5g (Saturated Fat 3g); Cholesterol 15mg; Sodium 45mg; Total Carbohydrate 15g (Dietary Fiber 0g); Protein 1g

Malted Madness Cookies

About 2 dozen cookies

Prep Time: **45 Minutes**   Start to Finish: **1 Hour**

COOKIES

1 cup packed brown sugar

½ cup butter or margarine, softened

2 eggs

2 cups all-purpose flour

½ cup chocolate-flavor malted milk powder

1 teaspoon baking powder

½ teaspoon baking soda

¼ teaspoon salt

GLAZE

1½ cups powdered sugar

¼ cup chocolate-flavor malted milk powder

2 to 3 tablespoons milk

½ teaspoon vanilla

1 cup chocolate-covered malted milk balls, crushed

1   Heat oven to 350°F. Grease cookie sheet with shortening or cooking spray. In large bowl, beat brown sugar, butter and eggs with electric mixer on medium speed, or mix with spoon, until well blended. Stir in flour, ½ cup malted milk powder, the baking powder, baking soda and salt.

2   On cookie sheet, drop dough by rounded tablespoonfuls about 2 inches apart.

3   Bake 12 to 15 minutes or until edges are set. Cool 1 minute; remove from cookie sheet to cooling rack. Cool completely, about 15 minutes.

4   In medium bowl, mix all glaze ingredients except crushed milk balls with spoon until smooth and spreadable. Spread glaze over cookies. Sprinkle with crushed candies.

1 Cookie: Calories 120 (Calories from Fat 30); Total Fat 4g (Saturated Fat 1g); Cholesterol 15mg; Sodium 110mg; Total Carbohydrate 21g (Dietary Fiber 0g); Protein 1g

> Need to plan ahead? Unbaked cookie dough can be frozen in an airtight container up to 9 months. Before baking, thaw frozen dough in the refrigerator at least 8 hours.

Fudge Crinkles { 2½ dozen cookies }

Prep Time: **1 Hour**   Start to Finish: **1 Hour**

1 box (1 lb 2.25 oz) devil's
food cake mix with pudding
in the mix

½ cup vegetable oil

2 eggs

1 teaspoon vanilla

⅓ cup powdered sugar

1 Heat oven to 350°F. In large bowl, mix cake mix, oil, eggs and
   vanilla with spoon until dough forms.

2 Shape dough into 1-inch balls. Roll balls in powdered sugar.
   On ungreased cookie sheet, place balls about 2 inches apart.

3 Bake 10 to 12 minutes or until set. Cool 1 minute; remove
   from cookie sheet to cooling rack. Cool completely, about
   30 minutes. Store tightly covered.

1 Cookie: Calories 110 (Calories from Fat 45); Total Fat 5g (Saturated Fat 1g); Cholesterol 15mg;
Sodium 140mg; Total Carbohydrate 15g (Dietary Fiber 0g); Protein 1g

{
Instead of rolling the cookies in powdered sugar, dip the tops
into chocolate candy sprinkles before baking.

For extra fun, stir 1 cup mini candy-coated chocolate baking
bits into the dough.
}

CLICK!

For another great chocolate lovers recipe
and on-line video, go to
www.bettycrocker.com/chocolava.

Mocha-Toffee Chocolate Cookies

About 5 dozen cookies

Prep Time: **1 Hour 10 Minutes**   Start to Finish: **1 Hour 10 Minutes**

4 teaspoons instant espresso
powder or instant coffee
granules

2 teaspoons vanilla

1 box (1 lb 2.25 oz) butter
recipe chocolate cake mix
with pudding in the mix

½ cup butter or margarine,
softened

2 eggs

1 cup miniature semisweet
chocolate chips

½ cup English toffee bits

1 Heat oven to 350°F. In small bowl, stir together coffee and
vanilla until coffee is dissolved. In large bowl, mix cake mix,
coffee mixture, butter and eggs with spoon until soft dough
forms. Stir in chocolate chips and toffee bits.

2 On ungreased cookie sheet, drop dough by rounded
teaspoonfuls about 2 inches apart.

3 Bake 7 to 10 minutes or until surface appears dry. Cool
1 minute; remove from cookie sheet to cooling rack.

1 Cookie: Calories 80 (Calories from Fat 35); Total Fat 4g (Saturated Fat 2g); Cholesterol 10mg;
Sodium 100mg; Total Carbohydrate 10g (Dietary Fiber 0g); Protein 0g

Who wants coffee? Enjoy a little extra jolt by gently pressing
one chocolate-covered coffee bean into the center of each
cookie before baking.

Choco-Hazelnut Latte Cookies

32 cookies

Prep Time: **50 Minutes**   Start to Finish: **1 Hour 10 Minutes**

1 pouch (1 lb 1.5 oz) sugar
cookie mix

⅓ cup unsweetened baking
cocoa

3 tablespoons instant coffee
granules or crystals

½ cup butter or margarine,
softened

3 tablespoons hazelnut-
flavored syrup for beverages
(from 12.7-oz bottle)

1 egg

1½ cups toasted hazelnuts,
chopped*

1 cup miniature semisweet
chocolate chips

⅔ cup chocolate creamy
ready-to-spread frosting
(from 1-lb container)

4½ teaspoons hazelnut-
flavored syrup for beverages
(from 12.7-oz bottle)

1   Heat oven to 350°F. In large bowl, stir together cookie mix,
cocoa and instant coffee. Add butter, 3 tablespoons syrup and
the egg; stir until soft dough forms. Stir in 1 cup of the nuts and
the chocolate chips.

2   On ungreased cookie sheets, drop dough with rounded
1½ tablespoon-size cookie scoop or by rounded tablespoonfuls
2 inches apart. Press each mound to flatten slightly.

3   Bake 8 to 10 minutes or until set. Cool 3 minutes; remove
from cookie sheets to cooling racks. Cool completely, about
15 minutes.

4   In small bowl, stir frosting and 4½ teaspoons syrup. Spread
about 1 teaspoon frosting on each cookie. Sprinkle with
remaining ½ cup nuts.

*To toast hazelnuts, heat oven to 350°F. Spread nuts in ungreased shallow
pan. Bake uncovered 6 to 10 minutes, stirring occasionally, until light brown.

1 Cookie: Calories 190; Total Fat 10g (Saturated Fat 3.5g); Sodium 85mg; Total Carbohydrate 22g
(Dietary Fiber 1g); Protein 2g

Chocolate Brownies

16 brownies

Prep Time: 25 Minutes   Start to Finish: **3 Hours 10 Minutes**

BROWNIES

⅔ cup butter or margarine

5 oz unsweetened baking chocolate, cut into pieces

1¾ cups granulated sugar

2 teaspoons vanilla

3 eggs

1 cup all-purpose flour*

1 cup chopped walnuts, if desired

CHOCOLATE BUTTERCREAM FROSTING, IF DESIRED

3 cups powdered sugar

⅓ cup unsweetened baking cocoa

⅓ cup butter or margarine, room temperature

2 teaspoons vanilla

3 to 4 tablespoons milk

1   Heat oven to 350°F. Spray the bottom and sides of a 9-inch square pan with the cooking spray.

2   In 1-quart saucepan, melt butter and chocolate over low heat, stirring constantly. Cool 5 minutes.

3   In medium bowl, beat granulated sugar, 2 teaspoons vanilla and the eggs with electric mixer on high speed 5 minutes. On low speed, beat in chocolate mixture, scraping bowl occasionally. Beat in flour just until mixed, scraping bowl occasionally. Stir in walnuts. Spread in pan.

4   Bake 40 to 45 minutes or just until brownies begin to pull away from sides of pan. Cool completely in pan on wire rack, about 2 hours.

5   Meanwhile, in medium bowl, beat the powdered sugar, cocoa and butter with a spoon or an electric mixer on low speed until well mixed. Stir in 2 teaspoons vanilla and 1 tablespoon of the milk. Gradually beat in just enough remaining milk to make frosting smooth and spreadable. Frost brownies. For brownies, cut into 4 rows by 4 rows.

*Do not use self-rising flour.

1 Brownie: Calories 310 (Calories from Fat 170); Total Fat 18g (Saturated Fat 8g); Cholesterol 60mg; Sodium 65mg; Total Carbohydrate 31g (Dietary Fiber 2g); Protein 4g

Double–Chocolate Chunk Brownies   24 brownies

Prep Time: **25 Minutes**   Start to Finish: **2 Hours**

BROWNIES
1 cup butter or margarine
1 cup granulated sugar
1 cup packed brown sugar
2 teaspoons vanilla
4 eggs
1¼ cups all-purpose flour
¾ cup baking cocoa
¼ teaspoon salt
1 cup semisweet chocolate chunks

6 oz white chocolate, chopped, or
  1 cup white vanilla baking chips

FROSTING
1½ cups powdered sugar
¼ cup baking cocoa
¼ cup butter or margarine, softened
2 to 3 tablespoons milk
3 oz white chocolate, chopped, or
  ½ cup white vanilla baking chips
1 teaspoon vegetable oil

1   Heat oven to 350°F. Grease bottom and sides of 13 × 9-inch pan with shortening or spray with cooking spray. In 4-quart saucepan, melt 1 cup butter over medium heat; remove from heat. Mix in granulated and brown sugar, vanilla and eggs until well blended. Stir in flour, ¾ cup cocoa and salt until well blended. Stir in semisweet chocolate and 6 oz white chocolate. Spread in pan.

2   Bake 30 to 35 minutes or until set. Cool completely, about 1 hour.

3   In large bowl, beat powdered sugar, ¼ cup cocoa, ¼ cup butter and enough of the milk with electric mixer on low speed until frosting is smooth and spreadable. Spread over brownies.

4   In microwavable container, microwave ½ cup white chocolate chunks and the oil uncovered on High 30 to 60 seconds, stirring once or twice, until thin enough to drizzle. When cool enough to handle, place in small resealable food-storage plastic bag; cut off tiny corner of bag. Squeeze bag to drizzle white chocolate over frosting. For brownies, cut into 6 rows by 4 rows.

1 Brownie: Calories 360 (Calories from Fat 170); Total Fat 19g (Saturated Fat 10g); Cholesterol 60mg; Sodium 120mg; Total Carbohydrate 46g (Dietary Fiber 2g); Protein 4g

For the best results, use semisweet chocolate chunks,
not chocolate chips.

Cookies 'n Creme Brownies

{ 20 brownies }

Prep Time: **25 Minutes**   Start to Finish: **2 Hour 25 Minutes**

1 box (1 lb 2.3 oz) fudge brownie mix

¼ cup water

⅔ cup vegetable oil

2 eggs

1 cup coarsely chopped creme-filled chocolate sandwich cookies (about 7 cookies)

½ cup powdered sugar

2 to 4 teaspoons milk

1   Heat oven to 350°F. Grease bottom only of 13 × 9-inch pan with shortening or spray bottom with cooking spray. In large bowl, stir brownie mix, water, oil and eggs until well blended. In pan, spread batter evenly. Sprinkle cookies over batter.

2   Bake 24 to 26 minutes or until toothpick inserted 2 inches from side of pan comes out almost clean. Cool completely, about 1 hour 30 minutes.

3   In small bowl, stir together powdered sugar and milk until smooth and thin enough to drizzle. Drizzle over brownies. For brownies, cut into 5 rows by 4 rows. Store covered at room temperature.

1 Brownie: Calories 340 (Calories from Fat 160); Total Fat 18g (Saturated Fat 5g); Cholesterol 45mg; Sodium 40mg; Total Carbohydrate 41g (Dietary Fiber 2g); Protein 4g

{ Change 'em up! With the variety of cookies available, you can easily substitute mint-flavored chocolate sandwich cookies, peanut butter chocolate sandwich cookies or double chocolate cookies to suit your taste. }

German Chocolate Bars | 48 bars

Prep Time: **15 Minutes**   Start to Finish: **3 Hours 55 Minutes**

½ cup butter or margarine, softened

1 box (1 lb 2.25 oz) German chocolate cake mix with pudding in the mix

1 container (1 lb) coconut pecan creamy ready-to-spread frosting

1 bag (6 oz) semisweet chocolate chips (1 cup)

¼ cup milk

1   Heat oven to 350°F. Lightly grease bottom and sides of 13 × 9-inch pan with shortening. In medium bowl, cut butter into cake mix, using pastry blender or crisscrossing 2 knives, until crumbly. Press half of the mixture (2½ cups) in bottom of pan. Bake 10 minutes.

2   Carefully spread frosting over baked layer; sprinkle evenly with chocolate chips. Stir milk into remaining cake mixture. Drop by teaspoonfuls onto chocolate chips.

3   Bake 25 to 30 minutes or until cake portion is slightly dry to the touch. Cool completely, about 1 hour. Cover and refrigerate about 2 hours or until firm. For bars, cut into 8 rows by 6 rows. Store covered in refrigerator.

1 Bar: Calories 135 (Calories from Fat 70); Fat 8g (Saturated 4g); Cholesterol 15mg; Sodium 100mg; Carbohydrate 15g (Dietary Fiber 0g); Protein 1g

For an easy dessert with restaurant style, place 2 bars on individual serving plates. Top with whipped cream and grated milk chocolate from a candy bar.

Chocolate-Caramel Bars | 24 bars |

Prep Time: **25 Minutes**   Start to Finish: **2 Hours 30 Minutes**

1 box (1 lb 2.25 oz) devil's
food cake mix with pudding
in the mix

¾ cup butter or margarine,
softened

1 egg

2 cups quick-cooking or old-
fashioned oats

1 bag (14 oz) vanilla caramels,
unwrapped

¼ cup milk

½ cup semisweet chocolate
chips

½ cup chopped pecans or
walnuts, if desired

1   Heat oven to 350°F (or 325°F if using dark or nonstick pan).
Generously grease bottom and sides of 13 × 9-inch pan with
shortening or cooking spray.

2   In large bowl, beat cake mix, butter and egg with electric mixer
on low speed until well blended. Stir in oats until crumbly (may
need to use hands to mix dough). Reserve 1½ cups cake mixture.
Press remaining mixture in pan (use plastic wrap or waxed paper
to press mixture if it is too sticky).

3   In heavy 2-quart saucepan, heat caramels and milk over
medium-low heat, stirring frequently, until melted. Pour over
chocolate layer in pan. Sprinkle with chocolate chips and
pecans. Sprinkle reserved cake mixture over top.

4   Bake 22 to 28 minutes or until caramel bubbles along edges and
cake mixture on top appears crisp and dry. Run knife around
sides of pan to loosen bars. Cool completely, about 1 hour 30
minutes. For bars, cut into 6 rows by 4 rows. Store covered at
room temperature.

1 Bar: Calories 250 (Calories from Fat 90); Total Fat 10g (Saturated Fat 5g); Cholesterol 25mg;
Sodium 250mg; Total Carbohydrate 37g (Dietary Fiber 2g); Protein 3g

{ Try milk chocolate or white vanilla baking chips instead
of semisweet chocolate chips for a different flavor
and appearance. }

Chocolate-Raspberry Cheesecake Bars | 48 bars |

Prep Time: **20 Minutes**   Start to Finish: **2 Hours 30 Minutes**

CRUST

1 box (1 lb 2.25 oz) devil's food cake mix with pudding in the mix

½ cup butter or margarine, softened

2 tablespoons milk

1 egg

1 cup raspberry pie filling (from 21-oz can)

CHEESECAKE FILLING

2 packages (8 oz each) cream cheese, softened

½ cup sour cream

½ cup sugar

1 teaspoon vanilla

2 eggs

1 tablespoon all-purpose flour

GARNISH

¼ cup semisweet chocolate chips

2 teaspoons shortening

48 fresh raspberries

1   Heat oven to 350°F (325°F for dark or nonstick pan). In large bowl, mix cake mix, butter, milk and 1 egg with spoon until dry ingredients are moistened. Spread in bottom of ungreased 15 × 10 × 1-inch pan. Spread raspberry pie filling over crust.

2   In large bowl, beat cream cheese, sour cream, sugar and vanilla with electric mixer on medium speed until smooth and creamy. Add 2 eggs, one at a time, beating after each until mixed. On low speed, beat in flour. Pour over pie filling.

3   Bake 30 to 38 minutes or until cheesecake filling is set. Cool completely, about 1 hour.

4   In microwavable food-storage plastic bag, place chocolate chips and shortening; seal bag. Microwave on High 15 seconds; squeeze bag. Microwave about 15 seconds longer or until melted; squeeze bag until chocolate is smooth. Cut off tiny corner of bag; squeeze bag to drizzle chocolate over bars. For bars, cut into 8 rows by 6 rows. Refrigerate 30 minutes before serving. Top each bar with fresh raspberry just before serving. Store in refrigerator.

1 Bar: Calories 130 (Calories from Fat 70); Total Fat 7g (Saturated Fat 4.5g); Cholesterol 30mg; Sodium 130mg; Total Carbohydrate 14g (Dietary Fiber 0g); Protein 2g

2

mix it up with chocolate

German Chocolate Picnic Cake

9 servings

Prep Time: **15 Minutes**   Start to Finish: **1 Hour 25 Minutes**

1¾ cups German chocolate cake mix with pudding in the mix (from 1 lb 2.25-oz box)

½ cup water

2 tablespoons vegetable oil

1 egg

½ cup packed brown sugar

⅓ cup all-purpose flour

⅓ cup quick-cooking or old-fashioned oats

3 tablespoons butter or margarine, softened

¾ teaspoon ground cinnamon

¼ teaspoon ground nutmeg

1 Heat oven to 350°F (325°F for dark or nonstick pan). Spray bottom only of 8- or 9-inch square pan with baking spray with flour.

2 In large bowl, beat cake mix, water, oil and egg with electric mixer on low speed 30 seconds. Beat on medium speed 2 minutes, scraping bowl occasionally. Pour batter into pan.

3 In medium bowl, stir remaining ingredients until well mixed; sprinkle evenly over batter in pan.

4 Bake 32 to 36 minutes or until toothpick inserted in center of cake comes out clean. Cool at least 30 minutes before serving. Serve warm or cool.

1 Serving: Calories 260 (Calories from Fat 90); Total Fat 10g (Saturated Fat 4g); Cholesterol 35mg; Sodium 260mg; Total Carbohydrate 41g (Dietary Fiber 1g); Protein 3g

{ If you plan to tote this cake to a picnic, bake it in a disposable foil pan. Then you don't have to carry home the dirty pan. }

Better-than-Almost-Anything Cake { 15 servings }

Prep Time: **10 Minutes**   Start to Finish: **3 Hours**

1 box (1 lb 2.25 oz) German chocolate cake mix with pudding in the mix

Water, vegetable oil and eggs called for on cake mix box

1 can (14 oz) sweetened condensed milk (not evaporated)

1 jar (16 to 17 oz) caramel, butterscotch or fudge topping

1½ cups whipping cream

¼ cup granulated or powdered sugar

1 cup toffee bits

1   Heat oven to 350°F (325°F for dark or nonstick pan). Generously grease bottom only of 13 × 9-inch pan with shortening.

2   Make and bake cake as directed on box, using water, oil and eggs. Cool 15 minutes.

3   With handle of wooden spoon, poke top of warm cake every ½ inch. Drizzle milk evenly over top of cake; let stand until milk has been absorbed into cake. Drizzle with caramel topping. Run knife around side of pan to loosen cake. Cover; refrigerate about 2 hours or until chilled.

4   In large bowl, beat whipping cream and sugar with electric mixer on high speed until soft peaks form. Spread over top of cake. Sprinkle with toffee bits. Store covered in refrigerator.

1 Serving: Calories 550 (Calories from Fat 230); Total Fat 25g (Saturated Fat 11g); Cholesterol 90mg; Sodium 490mg; Total Carbohydrate 75g (Dietary Fiber 1g); Protein 6g

{ One container (8 ounce) frozen whipped topping, thawed, can be substituted for the sweetened whipped cream. }

Chocolate–Cherry Cola Cake

12 servings

Prep Time: **30 Minutes**   Start to Finish: **2 Hours 15 Minutes**

1 jar (10 oz) maraschino cherries, drained, ¼ cup liquid reserved

1 box (1 lb 2.25 oz) devil's food cake mix with pudding in the mix

1 cup cherry cola carbonated beverage

½ cup vegetable oil

3 eggs

1 container (12 oz) vanilla whipped ready-to-spread frosting

1 cup marshmallow creme

24 maraschino cherries with stems, well drained, if desired

1   Heat oven to 350°F (325°F for dark or nonstick pan). Spray bottom only of 13 × 9-inch pan with baking spray with flour. Chop cherries; set aside.

2   In large bowl, beat cake mix, cola beverage, oil, eggs and ¼ cup reserved cherry liquid with electric mixer on low speed 30 seconds. Beat on medium speed 2 minutes. Stir in chopped cherries. Pour into pan.

3   Bake 35 to 43 minutes or until toothpick inserted in center comes out clean. Cool completely, about 1 hour.

4   In small bowl, mix frosting and marshmallow creme until smooth. Frost cake. Top each piece with 2 cherries.

1 Serving: Calories 480 (Calories from Fat 170); Total Fat 19g (Saturated Fat 5g); Cholesterol 55mg; Sodium 390mg; Total Carbohydrate 72g (Dietary Fiber 2g); Protein 4g

Cola Cake is an old southern recipe. This updated recipe uses a cake mix and cherry cola.

For chocolate-dipped cherries, melt ¼ cup semisweet chocolate chips and 1 teaspoon shortening in the microwave; stir. Dip well-drained cherries with stems into the chocolate; refrigerate to set.

Peppermint Pattie Poke Cake

15 servings

Prep Time: **25 Minutes**   Start to Finish: **3 Hours 15 Minutes**

CAKE

1 box (1 lb 2.25 oz) chocolate fudge cake mix with pudding in the mix

Water, vegetable oil and eggs called for on cake mix box

FILLING

1 box (4-serving size) white chocolate instant pudding and pie filling mix

2 cups milk

½ teaspoon peppermint extract

FROSTING

¼ teaspoon peppermint extract

1 container (12 oz) milk chocolate whipped ready-to-spread frosting

¾ cup coarsely chopped chocolate-covered peppermint patties (8 candies)

1 Heat oven to 350°F (325°F for dark or nonstick pan). Spray bottom only of 13 × 9-inch pan with baking spray with flour. Make and bake cake as directed on box for 13 × 9-inch pan. Cool 15 minutes. With handle of wooden spoon, poke top of warm cake every ½ inch.

2 In medium bowl, beat filling ingredients with whisk about 2 minutes. Immediately pour over cake. Cover loosely; refrigerate about 2 hours or until chilled.

3 Stir ¼ teaspoon peppermint extract into frosting. Spread frosting over top of cake. Sprinkle with peppermint patties. Store covered in refrigerator.

1 Serving: Calories 360 (Calories from Fat 130); Total Fat 15g (Saturated Fat 4.5g); Cholesterol 45mg; Sodium 440mg; Total Carbohydrate 54g (Dietary Fiber 1g); Protein 4g

To keep the candies from sticking together, sprinkle 1 tablespoon sugar over the cutting board. As you cut the candies, toss them with the sugar.

Vanilla instant pudding and pie filling mix can be used instead of the white chocolate pudding mix.

Chocolate Turtle Cake 20 servings

Prep Time: **30 Minutes**   Start to Finish: **2 Hours**

1 box (1 lb 2.25 oz) devil's food cake mix with pudding in the mix

Water, oil and eggs called for on cake mix box

1 bag (14 oz) caramels, unwrapped

½ cup evaporated milk

1 cup chopped pecans

1 cup semisweet chocolate chips (6 oz)

Ice cream or whipped cream, if desired

1   Heat oven to 350°F (325°F for dark or nonstick pans). Grease bottom and sides of 13 × 9-inch pan with shortening; lightly flour. Make cake mix as directed on box, using water, oil and eggs. Pour half of the batter into pan. Bake 22 minutes (25 minutes for dark or nonstick pans).

2   Meanwhile, in 1-quart saucepan, heat caramels and milk over medium heat about 10 minutes, stirring frequently, until caramels are melted.

3   Pour and spread caramel over warm cake in pan. Sprinkle with pecans and chocolate chips. Spread with remaining batter.

4   Bake 25 minutes (29 minutes for dark or nonstick pans). Place pan on cooling rack; run knife around sides of pan to loosen cake. Cool completely, about 1 hour. Serve with ice cream. Store tightly covered at room temperature.

1 Serving: Calories 340 (Calories from Fat 150); Total Fat 16g (Saturated Fat 5g); Cholesterol 35mg; Sodium 270mg; Total Carbohydrate 43g (Dietary Fiber 2g); Protein 4g

To melt the caramels in the microwave, put them in a 4-cup microwavable measuring cup with the milk and microwave uncovered on High 2 minutes to 3 minutes 30 seconds, stirring once or twice.

Make this cake even more indulgent by serving it with ice cream drizzled with chocolate and caramel topping. Sprinkle with additional chopped pecans.

Gooey Chocolate–Peanut Butter Cake [20 servings]

Prep Time: **25 Minutes**   Start to Finish: **1 Hour 45 Minutes**

1 box (1 lb 2.25 oz) devil's food cake mix with pudding in the mix

½ cup butter or margarine, softened

2 tablespoons milk

4 eggs

1 cup peanut butter chips (from 10-oz bag)

½ cup chopped roasted peanuts

1 package (8 oz) cream cheese, softened

½ cup peanut butter

1 teaspoon vanilla

3¾ cups powdered sugar

Hot fudge topping, if desired

Chopped peanuts, if desired

1 Heat oven to 350°F. Lightly spray 13 × 9-inch pan with baking spray with flour (do not use dark or nonstick pan). In large bowl, beat cake mix, butter, milk and 1 of the eggs with spoon until well mixed. Spread in pan. Sprinkle with peanut butter chips and peanuts.

2 In large bowl, beat cream cheese, peanut butter, vanilla and the remaining 3 eggs with electric mixer on medium speed until smooth. Beat in powdered sugar on low speed. Pour mixture over chocolate mixture in pan; spread evenly.

3 Bake 45 to 50 minutes or until topping is set and deep golden brown. Cool at least 30 minutes to serve warm, or cool completely. When cutting serving pieces, wipe knife with paper towel after cutting each row. Top each piece with hot fudge topping and chopped peanuts.

1 Serving: Calories 400 (Calories from Fat 170); Total Fat 19g (Saturated Fat 8g); Cholesterol 65mg; Sodium 370mg; Total Carbohydrate 50g (Dietary Fiber 2g); Protein 7g

{ This cake is more like a dessert square than a typical cake. Eat it with a fork. }

Chocolate Cupcakes with White Truffle Frosting   24 cupcakes

Prep Time: **35 Minutes**   Start to Finish: **1 Hour 10 Minutes**

1 box (1 lb 2.25 oz) devil's food cake mix with pudding in the mix

Water, vegetable oil and eggs called for on cake mix box

1 cup white vanilla baking chips (6 oz)

1 container (1 lb) vanilla or chocolate creamy ready-to-spread frosting

1   Heat oven to 350°F. Place paper baking cup in each of 24 regular-size muffin cups. Make and bake cake as directed on box for 24 cupcakes, using water, oil and eggs. Cool 10 minutes; remove from pan to cooling rack. Cool completely, about 30 minutes.

2   In medium microwavable bowl, microwave vanilla chips uncovered on Medium 4 to 5 minutes, stirring after 2 minutes. Stir until smooth; cool 5 minutes. Stir in frosting until well blended. Immediately frost cupcakes or pipe frosting onto cupcakes. Store loosely covered.

1 Cupcake: Calories 270 (Calories from Fat 120); Total Fat 13g (Saturated Fat 5g); Cholesterol 25mg; Sodium 240mg; Total Carbohydrate 36g (Dietary Fiber 0g)

Molten Chocolate Cupcakes

{ 18 cupcakes }

Prep Time: **30 Minutes**   Start to Finish: **2 Hours**

½ cup whipping cream

1 cup semisweet chocolate chips (6 oz)

1 box (1 lb 2.25 oz) devil's food cake mix with pudding in the mix

Water, vegetable oil and eggs called for on cake mix box

1 container (1 lb) chocolate creamy ready-to-spread frosting

Powdered sugar, if desired

Sliced strawberries, if desired

1 In 1-quart saucepan, heat whipping cream over medium-high heat until hot but not boiling. Stir in chocolate chips until melted and mixture is smooth. Refrigerate about 1 hour, stirring occasionally, until thick.

2 Heat oven to 350°F. Spray 18 large muffin cups with baking spray with flour. In large bowl, beat cake mix, water, oil and eggs with electric mixer on low speed 30 seconds; beat on medium speed 2 minutes, scraping bowl constantly. Divide batter evenly among muffin cups. Spoon 1 tablespoon cold chocolate mixture on top of batter in center of each cup.

3 Bake 18 to 22 minutes or until top springs back when lightly touched. Cool 1 minute. Carefully remove from pan; place on cooking parchment paper. Cool 10 minutes. Frost with chocolate frosting. Just before serving, dust with powdered sugar; garnish with strawberry slices. Serve warm.

1 Cupcake: Calories 340 (Calories from Fat 150); Total Fat 17g (Saturated Fat 6g); Cholesterol 45mg; Sodium 320mg; Total Carbohydrate 43g (Dietary Fiber 1g)

{ These warm, gooey cakes are delicious served with a small scoop of vanilla ice cream. }

Mud Slide Ice Cream Cake

15 servings

Prep Time: 30 Minutes   Start to Finish: 6 Hours

1 box (1 lb 2.25 oz) chocolate fudge cake mix with pudding in the mix

½ cup butter or margarine, melted

2 eggs

2 tablespoons coffee-flavored liqueur or prepared strong coffee

4 cups vanilla ice cream

1 container (12 oz) chocolate whipped ready-to-spread frosting

2 tablespoons coffee-flavored liqueur, if desired

1   Heat oven to 350°F (325°F for dark or nonstick pan). Spray bottom only of 13 × 9-inch pan with baking spray with flour.

2   In large bowl, beat cake mix, butter and eggs with electric mixer on medium speed until well blended. Spread batter in pan.

3   Bake 19 to 24 minutes or until center is set (top will appear dry and cracked). Cool completely, about 1 hour.

4   Brush 2 tablespoons liqueur over cake. Let ice cream stand at room temperature about 15 minutes to soften. Spread ice cream over cake. Freeze 3 hours or until firm.

5   In medium bowl, mix frosting and 2 tablespoons liqueur; spread over ice cream. Freeze at least 1 hour. Store covered in freezer.

1 Serving: Calories 390 (Calories from Fat 160); Total Fat 18g (Saturated Fat 9g); Cholesterol 60mg; Sodium 410mg; Total Carbohydrate 51g (Dietary Fiber 2g); Protein 4g

Coffee lovers can substitute coffee-flavored ice cream for the vanilla.

Black Forest Cake

12 servings

Prep Time: **25 Minutes**   Start to Finish: **2 Hours 15 Minutes**

CAKE

1 box (1 lb 2.25 oz) devil's food cake mix with pudding in the mix

Water, vegetable oil and eggs called for on cake mix box

FILLING AND TOPPING

1 pint (2 cups) whipping cream

½ cup powdered sugar

2 to 3 tablespoons brandy, if desired

1 can (21 oz) cherry pie filling

½ teaspoon almond extract

2 tablespoons sliced almonds

1   Heat oven to 350°F (325°F for dark or nonstick pans). Spray bottoms and sides of 2 (8- or 9-inch) round cake pans with baking spray with flour.

2   Make and bake cake as directed on box for 8- or 9-inch rounds, using water, oil and eggs. Cool 10 minutes; remove from pans to cooling rack. Cool completely, about 1 hour.

3   In medium bowl, beat whipping cream with electric mixer on high speed until slightly thickened. Gradually beat in powdered sugar until stiff peaks form. Fold in brandy. In another small bowl, mix pie filling and almond extract.

4   On serving plate, place 1 cake layer, bottom side up. Spread with 1 cup cherry mixture to within 1 inch of edge. Top with second cake layer, rounded side up. Frost top and side with whipped cream. Spoon remaining cherry mixture over top. Sprinkle with sliced almonds. Store covered in refrigerator.

1 Serving: Calories 390 (Calories from Fat 150); Total Fat 16g (Saturated Fat 4.5g); Cholesterol 60mg; Sodium 370mg; Total Carbohydrate 55g (Dietary Fiber 2g); Protein 5g

"Black Forest" usually describes desserts made with chocolate, cherries and whipping cream.

If you start with a chilled bowl, the whipping cream will whip up much faster.

Chocolate Mousse Brownie Dessert   12 to 16 servings

Prep Time: **15 Minutes**   Start to Finish: **2 Hours 20 Minutes**

¾ cup heavy whipping cream

1 bag (6 oz) semisweet chocolate chips (1 cup)

1 box (1 lb 2.4 oz) supreme brownie mix

Water, oil and eggs called for on brownie mix package

3 eggs

⅓ cup sugar

Whipping cream, if desired

1   Heat oven to 350°F. Grease bottom only of 13 × 9-inch pan with shortening.

2   In 2-quart saucepan, heat whipping cream and chocolate chips over low heat, stirring frequently, until chocolate is melted and mixture is smooth. Cool about 20 minutes.

3   Meanwhile, make brownie mix as directed on package, using water, oil and eggs. Spread batter in pan.

4   In small bowl, beat 3 eggs and sugar, using whisk or hand beater, until foamy. Stir into whipping cream mixture. Pour evenly over brownie batter.

5   Bake about 45 minutes or until topping is set. Cool completely, about 2 hours.

6   Serve at room temperature, or cover tightly and refrigerate until chilled. Top each serving with sweetened whipped cream. Store covered in refrigerator.

1 Serving: Calories 450 (Calories from Fat 200); Total Fat 23g (Saturated Fat 8g); Cholesterol 105mg; Sodium 200mg; Total Carbohydrate 55g (Dietary Fiber 3g); Protein 5g

Brownie Ice Cream Torte

16 servings

Prep Time: **25 Minutes**   Start to Finish: **3 Hours 25 Minutes**

1 box fudge brownie mix

Water, vegetable oil and eggs called for on brownie mix box

½ gallon vanilla ice cream, slightly softened

2 tablespoons pastel confetti candy sprinkles

16 red maraschino cherries with stems, drained

1 Heat oven to 350°F. Line two 9-inch round cake pans with foil; grease or spray bottoms only.

2 Make brownie batter as directed on box—except divide batter evenly between pans. Bake 22 to 26 minutes or until toothpick inserted 2 inches from side of pan comes out almost clean. Cool in pans about 1 hour or until completely cooled. Do not remove from pans.

3 Spread slightly softened ice cream evenly on brownies in pans. Freeze at least 2 hours or until ice cream is firm.

4 Remove desserts from pans; remove foil. Place on serving plates. Cut each dessert into 8 wedges. Decorate with candy sprinkles and cherries. Cover and freeze any remaining dessert.

1 Serving: Calories 370 (Calories from Fat 140); Total Fat 15g (Saturated Fat 6g); Cholesterol 60mg; Sodium 200mg; Total Carbohydrate 53g (Dietary Fiber 2g); Protein 5g

CLICK!

See how easy it is to make this torte by viewing the how-to video at www.bettycrocker.com/torte.

Triple-Chocolate Torte { 16 servings }

Prep Time: **15 Minutes**   Start to Finish: **6 Hours 35 Minutes**

1 box fudge brownie mix

¼ cup water

½ cup vegetable oil

2 eggs

1¼ cups milk

1 package (4-serving size) white chocolate instant pudding and pie filling mix

1 container (8 oz) frozen whipped topping, thawed

⅓ cup miniature semisweet chocolate chips

1 pint (2 cups) raspberries or strawberries, if desired

1 Heat oven to 325°F. Spray bottom only of 9-inch springform pan with cooking spray. Make brownie mix as directed on package, using water, oil and eggs. Spread in pan.

2 Bake 45 to 50 minutes or until toothpick inserted in center comes out clean. Cool completely, about 1 hour 30 minutes. (Do not remove side of pan.)

3 In large bowl, beat milk and pudding mix with whisk about 2 minutes or until thickened. Fold in whipped topping and chocolate chips. Pour over brownie.

4 Cover and freeze at least 4 hours before serving. Remove side of pan. Serve with raspberries. Store covered in freezer.

1 Serving: Calories 300 (Calories from Fat 120); Total Fat 14g (Saturated Fat 5g); Cholesterol 30mg; Sodium 230mg; Total Carbohydrate 42g (Dietary Fiber 2g); Protein 3g

{ Top pudding layer with finely chopped pistachio nuts for a little holiday color. }

3

chocolate delights

Chocolate Chip Snack Cake

{ 9 servings }

Prep Time: **10 Minutes**   Start to Finish: **1 Hour 5 Minutes**

1⅔ cups all-purpose flour

1 cup packed brown sugar or granulated sugar

¼ cup unsweetened baking cocoa

1 teaspoon baking soda

½ teaspoon salt

1 cup water

⅓ cup vegetable oil

1 teaspoon white vinegar

½ teaspoon vanilla

⅓ cup miniature chocolate chips

3 tablespoons granulated sugar

1   Heat oven to 350°F.

2   In ungreased 8-inch square pan, stir flour, brown sugar, cocoa, baking soda and salt with fork until well mixed. Stir in water, oil, vinegar and vanilla until well mixed. Spread batter evenly in pan and smooth top. Sprinkle with chocolate chips and granulated sugar.

3   Bake 35 to 40 minutes or until toothpick inserted in center comes out clean. To serve cake while warm, cool in pan on cooling rack 15 minutes; to serve it cool, let stand about 2 hours.

1 Serving: Calories 260 (Calories from Fat 80); Total Fat 9g (Saturated Fat 1.5g); Cholesterol 0mg; Sodium 280mg; Total Carbohydrate 43g (Dietary Fiber 1g); Protein 3g

Chocolate Snack Cake: Omit miniature chocolate chips and 3 tablespoons granulated sugar. After baking, sprinkle with powdered sugar before serving.

 CLICK!   For more great snack cake recipes, go to www.bettycrocker.com/snackcake.

Molten Chocolate Cakes { 6 servings }

Prep Time: **20 Minutes**   Start to Finish: **40 Minutes**

Unsweetened baking cocoa	3 egg yolks
6 oz semisweet baking chocolate, chopped	1½ cups powdered sugar
½ cup plus 2 tablespoons butter or margarine	½ cup all-purpose flour*
3 whole eggs	Additional powdered sugar, if desired
	Sugared kumquats, if desired

1 Heat oven to 450°F. Grease bottoms and sides of 6 (6-oz) custard cups with shortening; dust with cocoa. In 2-quart saucepan, melt chocolate and butter over low heat, stirring frequently. Cool slightly.

2 In large bowl, beat whole eggs and egg yolks with whisk or eggbeater until well blended. Beat in 1½ cups powdered sugar. Beat in melted chocolate mixture and the flour. Divide batter evenly among custard cups. Place cups on cookie sheet with sides.

3 Bake 12 to 14 minutes or until sides are set and centers are still soft (tops will be puffed and cracked). Let stand 3 minutes. Run small knife or metal spatula along sides of cakes to loosen. Immediately place heatproof serving plate upside down over each cup; turn plate and cup over. Remove cup. Sprinkle with additional powdered sugar. Garnish with kumquats. Serve warm.

*Do not use self-rising flour.

1 Serving: Calories 550 (Calories from Fat 300); Total Fat 33g (Saturated Fat 19g); Cholesterol 260mg; Sodium 170mg; Total Carbohydrate 56g (Dietary Fiber 2g); Protein 7g

{ Be sure to grease the custard cups with shortening, dust the cups with cocoa and bake the cakes at the correct oven temperature for the right time. These steps are critical to the success of this recipe. If the centers are too cakelike in texture, bake a few minutes less the next time; if they're too soft, bake a minute or two longer. }

German Chocolate Cake | 12 servings

Prep Time: **30 Minutes**   Start to Finish: **2 Hours 20 Minutes**

CAKE

4 oz sweet baking chocolate

½ cup water

2¼ cups all-purpose* or 2½ cups cake flour

1 teaspoon baking soda

1 teaspoon salt

2 cups granulated sugar

1 cup butter or margarine, softened

4 eggs

1 teaspoon vanilla

1 cup buttermilk

COCONUT-PECAN FILLING AND TOPPING

3 eggs

1 cup granulated sugar or packed brown sugar

½ cup butter or margarine (1 stick)

1 cup evaporated milk (from 12-oz can)

1 teaspoon vanilla

1⅓ cups flaked coconut

1 cup chopped pecans

1   Heat oven to 350°F. Grease bottom and side of three 8-inch or 9-inch round pans with shortening. Line bottoms of pans with waxed paper or cooking parchment paper.

2   In 1-quart saucepan, heat chocolate and water over low heat, stirring frequently, until chocolate is completely melted; cool.

3   In medium bowl, mix flour, baking soda and salt; set aside. In another medium bowl, beat 2 cups granulated sugar and 1 cup butter with electric mixer on high speed until light and fluffy. Separate 4 eggs; reserve egg whites. Beat egg yolks, one at a time, into sugar mixture. Beat in chocolate and 1 teaspoon vanilla on low speed. Beat flour mixture into sugar mixture alternately with buttermilk on low speed, beating just until smooth after each addition.

4   Wash and dry mixer beaters. In small bowl, beat reserved egg whites on high speed until stiff; fold into batter. Pour into pans. Refrigerate batter in third pan if not all pans will fit in oven at one time; bake third pan separately.

5   Bake 8-inch pans 35 to 40 minutes, 9-inch pans 30 to 35 minutes, or until toothpick inserted in center comes out clean. Cool 10 minutes; remove from pans to cooling rack. Remove waxed paper. Cool completely, about 1 hour.

6   Separate 3 eggs; save egg whites for another use. In 2-quart saucepan, stir egg yolks, 1 cup granulated sugar, ½ cup butter, the evaporated milk and 1 teaspoon vanilla until well mixed. Cook over medium heat about 12 minutes, stirring frequently, until thick and bubbly. Stir in coconut and pecans. Cool about 30 minutes, beating occasionally with spoon, until mixture is spreadable.

7   Fill layers and frost top of cake with coconut-pecan filling and topping, leaving side of cake unfrosted. Store covered in refrigerator.

*Do not use self-rising flour.

1 Serving: Calories 730 (Calories from Fat 360); Total Fat 40g (Saturated Fat 21g); Cholesterol 190mg; Sodium 550mg; Total Carbohydrate 83g (Dietary Fiber 2g); Protein 9g

Chocolate Malt Ice Cream Cake

[16 servings]

Prep Time: **30 Minutes**   Start to Finish: **7 Hours 5 Minutes**

1½ cups all-purpose flour

1 cup sugar

¼ cup unsweetened baking cocoa

1 teaspoon baking soda

½ teaspoon salt

⅓ cup vegetable oil

1 teaspoon white vinegar

1 teaspoon vanilla

1 cup water

1¼ cups chocolate fudge topping

1½ quarts (6 cups) vanilla ice cream, slightly softened

2 cups malted milk ball candies, coarsely chopped

1 cup whipping cream

Additional malted milk ball candies, if desired

1   Heat oven to 350°F. Grease bottom and side of 9- or 10-inch springform pan with shortening; lightly flour. In large bowl, mix flour, sugar, cocoa, baking soda and salt with spoon. Add oil, vinegar, vanilla and water; stir vigorously about 1 minute or until well blended. Immediately pour into pan.

2   Bake 30 to 35 minutes or until toothpick inserted in center comes out clean. Cool completely, about 1 hour.

3   Spread 1 cup of the fudge topping over cake. Freeze about 1 hour or until topping is firm.

4   In 3-quart bowl, mix ice cream and coarsely chopped candies; spread over cake. Freeze about 4 hours or until ice cream is firm.

5   In chilled medium bowl, beat whipping cream with electric mixer on high speed until stiff peaks form. Remove side of pan; place cake on serving plate. Top with whipped cream.

6   In small microwavable bowl, microwave remaining ¼ cup fudge topping uncovered on High 30 seconds or until thin enough to drizzle. Drizzle over whipped cream. Garnish with additional candies.

1 Serving: Calories 430 (Calories from Fat 180); Total Fat 20g (Saturated Fat 10g); Cholesterol 40mg; Sodium 310mg; Total Carbohydrate 58g (Dietary Fiber 2g); Protein 5g

{ Love chocolate? Use chocolate ice cream instead of vanilla. }

Best Chocolate Cake with Fudge Frosting

12 to 16 servings

Prep Time: **20 Minutes**   Start to Finish: **2 Hours 15 Minutes**

CHOCOLATE CAKE

2 cups all-purpose flour

2 cups sugar

½ cup shortening

¾ cup water

¾ cup buttermilk

1 teaspoon baking soda

1 teaspoon salt

1 teaspoon vanilla

½ teaspoon baking powder

2 eggs

4 oz unsweetened chocolate, melted, cooled

FUDGE FROSTING

2 cups sugar

½ cup shortening

3 oz unsweetened chocolate

⅔ cup milk

½ teaspoon salt

2 teaspoons vanilla

1   Heat oven to 350°F. Grease and flour 13 × 9-inch pan, 3 (8-inch) round pans or 2 (9-inch) round pans.

2   In large bowl, beat all cake ingredients with electric mixer on low speed 30 seconds, scraping bowl constantly. Beat on high speed 3 minutes, scraping bowl occasionally. Pour into pan(s).

3   Bake rectangular pan 40 to 45 minutes, round pans 30 to 35 minutes, or until toothpick inserted in center comes out clean. Cool round pans 10 minutes; remove from pans to cooling rack. Cool completely.

4   Mix all frosting ingredients except vanilla in 2½-quart saucepan. Heat to rapid boil, stirring occasionally. Boil 1 minute without stirring. Place saucepan in bowl of ice and water. Beat until frosting is smooth and of spreading consistency. Stir in vanilla.

5   Frost cake. Fill layers with ⅓ cup frosting; frost side and top with remaining frosting.

1 Serving: Calories 620 (Calories from Fat 250); Fat 28g (Saturated 10g); Cholesterol 40mg; Sodium 450mg; Carbohydrate 89g (Dietary Fiber 3g); Protein 6g

Chocolate Cake à l'Orange

{ 12 servings }

Prep Time: **40 Minutes**   Start to Finish: **2 Hours 35 Minutes**

CAKE

2 oz unsweetened baking chocolate

1 cup butter or margarine

1 cup granulated sugar

1 cup sour cream

2 tablespoons grated orange peel

2 teaspoons vanilla

3 eggs

1½ cups all-purpose flour

1 teaspoon baking powder

1 teaspoon baking soda

¼ teaspoon salt

GLAZE AND GARNISH

1 oz unsweetened baking chocolate

2 tablespoons butter or margarine

⅓ cup powdered sugar

1 to 2 tablespoons fresh orange juice

Orange peel strips

1   Heat oven to 350°F. Grease 12-cup fluted tube cake pan with shortening; lightly flour. In small microwavable bowl, microwave 2 oz chocolate uncovered on High 1 minute. Stir; microwave in 30-second increments, stirring after each, until melted. Set aside to cool slightly.

2   In large bowl, beat 1 cup butter and the granulated sugar with electric mixer on medium speed until blended. Beat in melted chocolate. Add sour cream, orange peel, vanilla and eggs; beat until well blended. On low speed, beat in remaining cake ingredients. Spread batter in pan.

3   Bake 30 to 40 minutes or until toothpick inserted in center comes out clean. Cool 15 minutes. Remove from pan to cooling rack. Cool completely, about 1 hour.

4   In 1-quart saucepan, heat 1 oz chocolate and 2 tablespoons butter over low heat 2 to 3 minutes, stirring occasionally, until melted. Remove from heat. With whisk, beat in powdered sugar and 1 tablespoon of the orange juice. Beat in additional orange

juice, 1 teaspoon at a time, until glaze is smooth and consistency of thick syrup. Drizzle glaze over cake, allowing some to run down side. Garnish with orange peel strips.

1 Serving: Calories 400 (Calories from Fat 240); Total Fat 26g (Saturated Fat 16g); Cholesterol 110mg; Sodium 340mg; Total Carbohydrate 36g (Dietary Fiber 2g); Protein 5g

Chocolate Cake with Raspberry Sauce { 12 servings }

Prep Time: **25 Minutes**   Start to Finish: **2 Hours 5 Minutes**

CAKE

1 cup semisweet chocolate chips (6 oz)

½ cup butter or margarine

½ cup all-purpose flour

4 eggs, separated

½ cup sugar

SAUCE

1 box (10 oz) frozen raspberries, thawed, drained and juice reserved

¼ cup sugar

2 tablespoons cornstarch

1 to 2 tablespoons orange- or raspberry-flavored liqueur, if desired

GLAZE

½ cup semisweet chocolate chips

2 tablespoons butter or margarine

2 tablespoons light corn syrup

GARNISH

½ cup whipped cream

Fresh raspberries, if desired

1   Heat oven to 325°F. Grease bottom and side of 8-inch springform pan or 9-inch round cake pan with shortening. In 2-quart heavy saucepan, melt 1 cup chocolate chips and ½ cup butter over medium heat, stirring occasionally. Cool 5 minutes. Stir in flour until smooth. Stir in egg yolks until well blended; set aside.

2   In large bowl, beat egg whites with electric mixer on high speed until foamy. Beat in ½ cup sugar, 1 tablespoon at a time, until soft peaks form. Using rubber spatula, fold chocolate mixture into egg whites. Spread in pan.

3   Bake springform pan 35 to 40 minutes, round cake pan 30 to 35 minutes, or until toothpick inserted in center comes out clean (top will appear dry and cracked). Cool 10 minutes. Run knife along side of cake to loosen; remove side of springform pan. Place cooling rack upside down over cake; turn rack and cake over. Remove bottom of springform pan or round cake pan. Cool completely, about 1 hour.

4   Meanwhile, add enough water to reserved raspberry juice to measure 1 cup. In 1-quart saucepan, mix ¼ cup sugar and the cornstarch. Stir in juice and thawed raspberries. Heat to boiling over medium heat. Boil and stir 1 minute. Place small strainer over small bowl. Pour mixture through strainer to remove seeds; discard seeds. Stir liqueur into mixture; set aside.

5   Place cake on serving plate. In 1-quart saucepan, heat glaze ingredients over medium heat, stirring occasionally, until chocolate chips are melted. Spread over top of cake, allowing some to drizzle down side. Place whipped cream in decorating bag fitted with star tip. Pipe a rosette onto each serving. Serve cake with sauce. Garnish with fresh raspberries.

1 Serving: Calories 360 (Calories from Fat 190); Total Fat 21g (Saturated Fat 12g); Cholesterol 105mg; Sodium 100mg; Total Carbohydrate 40g (Dietary Fiber 2g); Protein 4g

Be as creative as you like with the chocolate glaze! Drizzle it over the cake using a fork, or place it in a food-storage plastic bag and squeeze it through a snipped-off corner.

CLICK!   See how easy it is to make and freeze whipped cream by viewing the how-to video at www.bettycrocker.com/whippedcream.

Chocolate Chip–Toffee Cheesecake | 12 servings

Prep Time: **30 Minutes**   Start to Finish: **5 Hours 45 Minutes**

CRUST

1¼ cups finely crushed chocolate graham crackers (18 squares)

2 tablespoons sugar

¼ cup butter or margarine, melted

FILLING

2 packages (8 oz each) cream cheese, softened

½ cup sugar

1 teaspoon vanilla

2 eggs

2 cups milk chocolate-coated toffee bits (from two 8-oz bags)

TOPPING

½ cup semisweet chocolate chips

2 tablespoons whipping cream

1 Heat oven to 300°F. In medium bowl, mix crumbs, 2 tablespoons sugar and the butter. In ungreased 9-inch springform pan, press crumb mixture in bottom and 1 to 1½ inches up side.

2 In large bowl, beat cream cheese, ½ cup sugar and the vanilla with electric mixer on medium speed until smooth. Add eggs, one at a time, beating until smooth after each addition. Reserve 2 tablespoons of the toffee bits for garnish; gently stir remaining toffee bits into cream cheese mixture. Pour mixture into crust.

3 Bake 50 to 60 minutes or until set. Turn off oven; leave door open 4 inches. Cool cheesecake in oven 30 minutes.

4 Remove cheesecake from oven; place on cooling rack. Without releasing or removing side of pan, run metal spatula carefully along side of cheesecake to loosen. Cool 30 minutes. Run metal spatula along side of cheesecake to loosen again. Refrigerate uncovered until thoroughly chilled, at least 3 hours.

5 In small microwavable bowl, microwave chocolate chips and whipping cream uncovered on High 20 to 30 seconds or until chips are melted and can be stirred smooth. Cool 5 minutes. Spread topping evenly over top of cheesecake. Sprinkle reserved 2 tablespoons toffee bits around outer edge. Refrigerate until topping is set, about 15 minutes. Remove side of pan before serving.

1 Serving: Calories 480 (Calories from Fat 290); Total Fat 33g (Saturated Fat 20g); Cholesterol 100mg; Sodium 290mg; Total Carbohydrate 41g (Dietary Fiber 1g); Protein 6g

White Chocolate Cheesecake

16 servings

Prep Time: **45 Minutes**   Start to Finish: **10 Hours 45 Minutes**

CRUST AND FILLING
1 cup crushed chocolate wafer cookies

2 tablespoons butter or margarine, melted

3 packages (8 oz each) cream cheese, softened

½ cup sugar

3 eggs

1 teaspoon vanilla

1 bag (12 oz) white vanilla baking chips (2 cups), melted

½ cup half-and-half

SAUCE
½ cup cranberry juice cocktail

2 tablespoons sugar

2 teaspoons cornstarch

1 package (12 oz) frozen raspberries, thawed, juice reserved

1   Heat oven to 325°F. In small bowl, mix crushed cookies and butter. Press evenly in bottom of ungreased 9- or 10-inch springform pan. Refrigerate while making filling.

2   In large bowl, beat cream cheese with electric mixer on medium speed until smooth. Gradually beat in ½ cup sugar until smooth. Beat in eggs, one at a time. Beat in vanilla, melted chips and half-and-half until blended. Pour over crust; smooth top.

3   Bake 55 to 60 minutes or until center is set. Cool 30 minutes. Cover and refrigerate at least 8 hours.

4   In 1-quart saucepan, mix cranberry juice cocktail, 2 tablespoons sugar and the cornstarch. Cook over medium heat, stirring constantly, until mixture thickens and boils. Remove from heat; cool 30 minutes. Stir in raspberries and reserved juice. Cool completely.

5   Run metal spatula along side of cheesecake to loosen; remove side of pan. Serve cheesecake with sauce. Store cheesecake and sauce covered in refrigerator.

1 Serving: Calories 350 (Calories from Fat 190); Total Fat 21g (Saturated Fat 13g); Cholesterol 85mg; Sodium 250mg; Total Carbohydrate 34g (Dietary Fiber 2g); Protein 8g

This is a great recipe to make ahead of time. Cover the cooled cheesecake with foil and refrigerate no longer than 3 days. Cover and refrigerate the sauce no longer than 2 days.

Cinnamon-Almond-Chocolate Tart

8 servings

Prep Time: **15 Minutes**   Start to Finish: **1 Hour 35 Minutes**

ALMOND CRUST
1 cup all-purpose flour
2 tablespoons sugar
1 cup slivered almonds
½ cup butter or margarine, softened
1 egg

FILLING
½ cup sugar
1 teaspoon ground cinnamon

1 tablespoon corn syrup
⅛ teaspoon almond extract
3 eggs
3 oz semisweet baking chocolate, melted, cooled
6 tablespoons butter or margarine, melted

GARNISH, IF DESIRED
Whipped cream
Additional ground cinnamon

1   Heat oven to 350°F. In food processor or blender, place flour, 2 tablespoons sugar and the almonds. Cover; process until almonds are finely chopped. Add ½ cup butter and the egg. Cover; process until well blended. Press mixture in bottom and ½ inch up side of ungreased 9-inch tart pan with removable bottom.

2   Bake 20 to 25 minutes or until light brown. If crust puffs while baking, poke with fork.

3   Meanwhile, in medium bowl, beat ½ cup sugar, 1 teaspoon cinnamon, the corn syrup, almond extract and 3 eggs with whisk until smooth. Stir in chocolate and 6 tablespoons butter.

4   Pour filling into hot crust. Bake 18 to 24 minutes or until almost set in center. Cool on cooling rack at least 30 minutes before serving.

5   Remove side of pan. Serve tart topped with whipped cream; sprinkle with additional cinnamon. Store covered in refrigerator.

1 Serving: Calories 490 (Calories from Fat 300); Total Fat 33g (Saturated Fat 16g); Cholesterol 160mg; Sodium 180mg; Total Carbohydrate 39g (Dietary Fiber 3g); Protein 8g

{ Serve this cinnamon- and almond-flavored tart with a scoop of cinnamon ice cream. }

Chocolate Dream Tart | 12 to 16 servings

Prep Time: **10 Minutes**   Start to Finish: **1 Hour 50 Minutes**

⅓ cup butter or margarine, softened

1 cup all-purpose flour

1 egg

1 tablespoon butter or margarine

1 can (14 oz) sweetened condensed milk

1 bag (12 oz) semisweet chocolate chips (2 cups)

½ cup chopped walnuts

1 teaspoon vanilla

Unsweetened whipped cream, if desired

1 Heat oven to 400°F. In medium bowl, cut ⅓ cup butter into flour, using pastry blender (or pulling 2 table knives through ingredients in opposite directions), until mixture is crumbly. Stir in egg until dough forms. Press firmly and evenly against bottom and side of ungreased 9-inch tart pan with removable bottom. Bake 12 to 15 minutes or until golden brown; cool in pan on wire rack.

2 Reduce oven temperature to 350°F. In 2-quart saucepan, melt 1 tablespoon butter over low heat. Stir in milk and chocolate chips. Cook over low heat, stirring occasionally, until chocolate is melted. Stir in walnuts and vanilla. Spread in baked crust.

3 Bake about 25 minutes or until edge is set but chocolate appears moist in center. Cool completely in pan on wire rack, about 1 hour. To serve, top each slice with whipped cream.

1 Serving: Calories 390 (Calories from Fat 190); Total Fat 21g (Saturated Fat 10g); Cholesterol 45mg; Sodium 90mg; Total Carbohydrate 45g (Dietary Fiber 2g); Protein 6g

{ To show off this sinfully rich dessert, garnish with chocolate curls or dip ends of toasted walnut halves into melted chocolate and place on each serving with dollop of whipped cream. }

Chocolate Truffle Pie   { 12 servings }

Prep Time: **25 Minutes**   Start to Finish: **3 Hours**

CRUST

1 ¼ cups chocolate cookie crumbs

¼ cup butter or margarine, melted

FILLING

1 bag (12 oz) semisweet chocolate chips (2 cups)

½ pint (1 cup) whipping cream

1 teaspoon vanilla

2 egg yolks

TOPPING

½ cup whipping cream

1 tablespoon powdered sugar

Unsweetened baking cocoa, if desired

1   In small bowl, mix cookie crumbs and butter. In ungreased 9-inch glass pie plate, press crumb mixture in bottom and 1 inch up side.

2   In double boiler set over hot simmering water, heat chocolate chips 2 to 3 minutes, stirring frequently, until melted and smooth. Gradually add 1 cup whipping cream, stirring constantly, until combined. Stir in vanilla and egg yolks until well blended. Cook over medium-low heat 5 to 6 minutes, stirring frequently, until thickened and hot. Pour filling into crust. Refrigerate at least 3 hours or until firm.

3   In medium bowl, beat ½ cup whipping cream and the powdered sugar with electric mixer on high speed 1 to 2 minutes or until soft peaks form. Top individual servings with whipped cream. Dust with cocoa.

1 Serving: Calories 350 (Calories from Fat 220); Total Fat 24g (Saturated Fat 14g); Cholesterol 80mg; Sodium 125mg; Total Carbohydrate 30g (Dietary Fiber 2g); Protein 3g

To evenly press the crumb mixture into the pie plate, use the bottom of a dry measuring cup.

Don't own a double boiler? Place a small saucepan in a larger skillet or saucepan filled with 1 to 2 inches of simmering water.

chocolate bites and more

Luscious Chocolate Truffles

{ About 24 candies }

Prep Time: **20 Minutes**   Start to Finish: **1 Hour 25 Minutes**

1 bag (12 oz) semisweet
chocolate chips (2 cups)

2 tablespoons butter or
margarine

¼ cup heavy whipping cream

2 tablespoons liqueur
(almond, cherry, coffee,
hazelnut, Irish cream,
orange, raspberry, etc.),
if desired

1 tablespoon shortening

Finely chopped nuts,
if desired

¼ cup powdered sugar,
if desired

½ teaspoon milk, if desired

1   Line cookie sheet with foil. In heavy 2-quart saucepan, melt 1
cup of the chocolate chips over low heat, stirring constantly;
remove from heat. Stir in butter. Stir in whipping cream and
liqueur. Refrigerate 10 to 15 minutes, stirring frequently, just
until thick enough to hold a shape.

2   Drop mixture by teaspoonfuls onto foil. Shape into balls. (If
mixture is too sticky, refrigerate until firm enough to shape.)
Freeze 30 minutes.

3   In 1-quart saucepan, heat shortening and remaining 1 cup
chocolate chips over low heat, stirring constantly, until chocolate
is melted and mixture is smooth; remove from heat. Using fork,
dip truffles, one at a time, into chocolate. Return to foil-covered
cookie sheet. Immediately sprinkle some of the truffles with
nuts. Refrigerate about 10 minutes or until coating is set.

4 In small bowl, stir powdered sugar and milk until smooth; drizzle over some of the truffles. Refrigerate just until set. Store in airtight container in refrigerator. Serve truffles at room temperature by removing from refrigerator about 30 minutes before serving.

1 Truffle: Calories 100 (Calories from Fat 60); Total Fat 7g (Saturated Fat 3.5g); Cholesterol 5mg; Sodium 10mg; Total Carbohydrate 9g (Dietary Fiber 0g); Protein 0g

Milk Chocolate Truffles: Substitute 1 cup milk chocolate chips for the 1 cup of semisweet chocolate chips in step 1.

Toffee Truffles: Stir 3 tablespoons chopped chocolate-covered English toffee candy into whipping cream mixture.

White and Dark Chocolate Truffles: Stir 3 tablespoons chopped white chocolate baking bar into whipping cream mixture.

{ For the ultimate in decadent gifts, put together a montage of all four flavors, as pictured on the cover. }

See photo on cover.

Dark Chocolate–Hazelnut Truffles

36 truffles

Prep Time: **30 Minutes** Start to Finish: **2 Hours 40 Minutes**

4 oz bittersweet baking chocolate, chopped

4 oz semisweet baking chocolate, chopped

¼ cup whipping cream

5 tablespoons cold butter, cut into pieces

2 tablespoons hazelnut liqueur

4 oz (about 1 cup) hazelnuts (filberts)

1 In 1-quart heavy saucepan, heat both chocolates and whipping cream over low heat, stirring constantly, until chocolate is melted and smooth. Remove from heat. Stir in butter, a few pieces at a time. Stir in liqueur. Place plastic wrap over surface of chocolate. Refrigerate about 2 hours, stirring once, until firm enough to hold its shape.

2 Meanwhile, heat oven to 350°F. Place hazelnuts in ungreased shallow pan. Bake 6 to 10 minutes, stirring occasionally, until light brown. Rub with towel to remove skins. Cool 10 minutes. Place nuts in food processor. Cover; process with on-and-off pulses 20 to 30 seconds or until finely ground. Place on sheet of waxed paper.

3 Scoop rounded teaspoonfuls of chocolate mixture onto nuts. Roll lightly to coat and shape into 1-inch balls (truffles do not need to be smooth; they should be a little rough). Place on plate; cover loosely. Store loosely covered in refrigerator. Let stand at room temperature 15 minutes before serving.

1 Truffle: Calories 70 (Calories from Fat 50); Total Fat 6g (Saturated Fat 3g); Cholesterol 5mg; Sodium 15mg; Total Carbohydrate 3g (Dietary Fiber 1g); Protein 0g

For added "aah," place each truffle in a small paper candy cup.

Black-and-White Truffles

About 72 truffles

Prep Time: **30 Minutes**   Start to Finish: **1 Hour 45 Minutes**

1 package (1 lb 2 oz) creme-filled chocolate sandwich cookies

1 package (8 oz) cream cheese, softened

36 oz (from two 24-oz packages) vanilla-flavored candy coating (almond bark)

½ cup semisweet chocolate chips

½ teaspoon vegetable oil

1   Line 2 cookie sheets with waxed paper. Place cookies in large food processor. Cover; process with on-and-off pulses until consistency of fine crumbs. In large bowl, stir cookie crumbs and cream cheese until well blended and mixture forms a doughlike consistency.

2   Chop 8 oz of the candy coating; stir into dough mixture. Roll dough into 1-inch balls; place half on each cookie sheet. Freeze about 30 minutes or until very firm.

3   In small microwavable bowl, microwave half of remaining 28 oz candy coating on High 1 minute 30 seconds; stir. Continue microwaving and stirring in 15-second intervals until melted and smooth.

4   Remove half of the balls from freezer. Using 2 forks, dip and roll each ball in coating; return to cookie sheet. Melt remaining candy coating; dip remaining balls.

5   In 1-quart resealable freezer plastic bag, place chocolate chips and oil; seal bag. Microwave on High 35 to 50 seconds, squeezing chips in bag every 15 seconds, until chips are melted and mixture is smooth. Cut small tip from bottom corner of each bag. Drizzle chocolate over truffles. Refrigerate 30 to 45 minutes or until chocolate is set. Store covered in refrigerator.

1 Truffle: Calories 130 (Calories from Fat 70); Total Fat 7g (Saturated Fat 4g); Cholesterol 5mg; Sodium 60mg; Total Carbohydrate 14g (Dietary Fiber 0g); Protein 1g

Raspberry Truffle Cups { 24 truffle cups }

Prep Time: **30 Minutes**   Start to Finish: **1 Hour 35 Minutes**

6 oz vanilla-flavored candy coating (almond bark), cut into pieces

6 oz semisweet baking chocolate, cut into pieces

2 tablespoons butter or margarine, cut into pieces

⅓ cup whipping cream

2 tablespoons raspberry-flavored liqueur or raspberry pancake syrup

24 fresh raspberries

1 Melt candy coating as directed on package. Spread 1 teaspoon coating evenly in bottom and up side of each of 24 miniature paper candy cups. Let stand until hardened.

2 In 2-quart saucepan, melt chocolate over low heat, stirring constantly. Remove from heat. Stir in remaining ingredients except raspberries. Refrigerate about 35 minutes, stirring frequently, until mixture is thickened and mounds when dropped from a spoon.

3 Place raspberry in each candy-coated cup. Spoon chocolate mixture into decorating bag with star tip. Pipe mixture into candy-coated cups over raspberry. Place cups on cookie sheet. Refrigerate until chocolate mixture is firm, about 30 minutes. If desired, peel paper from truffle cups before serving. Store tightly covered in refrigerator.

1 Truffle Cup: Calories 100 Calories from Fat 60); Total Fat 6g (Saturated Fat 4g); Cholesterol 10mg; Sodium 15mg; Total Carbohydrate 9g (Dietary Fiber 0g); Protein 0g

Crème de Menthe Truffle Cups: Add ¼ cup finely ground almonds to the chocolate mixture and substitute crème de menthe for the raspberry liqueur.

Cherry Truffle Cups: Substitute cherry-flavored liqueur for the raspberry liqueur and 24 candied cherry halves for the raspberries.

Minty Fudge Cups

24 fudge cups

Prep Time: **30 Minutes**   Start to Finish: **1 Hour 20 Minutes**

TOPPING

1 package (4.67 oz)
rectangular chocolate
mints, unwrapped

MINTY FUDGE FILLING

⅔ cup granulated sugar

⅓ cup unsweetened baking
cocoa

2 tablespoons butter or
margarine, softened

1 egg

Reserved ½ cup coarsely
chopped mints

FUDGE CUPS

¼ cup butter or margarine,
softened

1 package (3 oz) cream
cheese, softened

¾ cup all-purpose flour

¼ cup powdered sugar

2 tablespoons unsweetened
baking cocoa

½ teaspoon vanilla

1 container (1 lb) chocolate
creamy ready-to-spread
frosting

1 Heat oven to 350°F. Place paper baking cup in each of 24 mini
muffin cups. Coarsely chop enough mints (about 15) to measure
½ cup; reserve for filling. Coarsely chop remaining mints for
topping; set aside.

2 In small bowl, beat all filling ingredients except chopped mints
with spoon until well mixed; stir in mints.

3 In large bowl, beat ¼ cup butter and the cream cheese with
electric mixer on medium speed, or mix with spoon. Stir in
flour, powdered sugar, 2 tablespoons cocoa and the vanilla.

4 Shape dough into 1-inch balls. Press each ball in bottom and up
side of each muffin cup. Spoon about 2 teaspoons filling into
each cup.

5 Bake 18 to 20 minutes or until almost no indentation remains
when filling is touched lightly. Cool slightly; carefully remove from
muffin cups to cooling rack. Cool completely, about 30 minutes.
Frost with frosting. Sprinkle with remaining chopped mints.

1 Fudge Cup: Calories 205 (Calories from Fat 100); Total Fat 11g (Saturated Fat 7g); Cholesterol
20mg; Sodium 40mg; Total Carbohydrate 25g (Dietary Fiber 1g)

Chocolate Fudge [64 candies]

Prep Time: **10 Minutes** Start to Finish: **2 Hours 35 Minutes**

4 cups sugar

1⅓ cups milk or half-and-half

¼ cup corn syrup

¼ teaspoon salt

4 oz unsweetened baking chocolate or ⅔ cup baking cocoa

¼ cup butter or margarine

2 teaspoons vanilla

1 cup coarsely chopped nuts, if desired

1   Grease bottom and sides of 8-inch square pan with butter.

2   In 3-quart saucepan, cook sugar, milk, corn syrup, salt and chocolate over medium heat, stirring constantly, until chocolate is melted and sugar is dissolved. Cook, stirring occasionally, to 234°F on candy thermometer or until small amount of mixture dropped into cup of very cold water forms a soft ball that flattens when removed from water; remove from heat. Stir in butter.

3   Cool mixture without stirring to 120°F, about 1 hour. (Bottom of saucepan will be lukewarm.) Add vanilla. Beat vigorously and continuously with wooden spoon 5 to 10 minutes or until mixture is thick and no longer glossy. (Mixture will hold its shape when dropped from a spoon.)

4   Quickly stir in nuts. Spread in pan. Let stand about 1 hour or until firm. Cut into 1-inch squares.

1 Candy: Calories 80 (Calories from Fat 15); Total Fat 2g (Saturated Fat 1g); Cholesterol 0mg; Sodium 20mg; Total Carbohydrate 14g (Dietary Fiber 0g); Protein 0g

Chocolate-Dipped Strawberries

18 to 20 strawberries

Prep Time: **20 Minutes**   Start to Finish: **50 Minutes**

1 pint (2 cups) medium-large
strawberries (18 to
20 strawberries)

½ cup semisweet chocolate
chips or white vanilla
baking chips

1 teaspoon shortening or
vegetable oil

1   Gently rinse strawberries and dry on paper towels (berries must
    be completely dry). Line cookie sheet with waxed paper.

2   In 1-quart saucepan, melt chocolate chips and shortening over
    low heat, stirring frequently. Remove from heat.

3   Dip lower half of each strawberry into chocolate mixture; allow
    excess to drip back into saucepan. Place on waxed paper–lined
    tray or cookie sheet.

4   Refrigerate uncovered about 30 minutes or until chocolate is
    firm, or until ready to serve. Store covered in refrigerator so
    chocolate does not soften (if made with oil, chocolate will soften
    more quickly at room temperature).

1 Strawberry: Calories 30 (Calories from Fat 20); Total Fat 2g (Saturated Fat 1g); Cholesterol 0mg;
Sodium 0mg; Total Carbohydrate 4g (Dietary Fiber 1g); Protein 0g

CLICK!   See how easy it is to make the strawberries
by viewing the how-to video at www
.bettycrocker.com/strawberries.

Milk Chocolate Fondue

8 servings

Prep Time: **15 Minutes**   Start to Finish: **15 Minutes**

⅔ cup half-and-half

12 oz milk chocolate or 1 bag (11.5 oz) milk chocolate chips (2 cups)

2 tablespoons orange-flavored liqueur, kirsch, brandy or half-and-half

Dippers (pound cake cubes, strawberries, pineapple chunks, apple slices, marshmallows)

1 In heavy 2-quart saucepan, heat half-and-half and chocolate over low heat, stirring constantly, until chocolate is melted and mixture is smooth; remove from heat. Stir in liqueur. Pour into fondue pot or chafing dish.

2 Spear dippers with fondue forks; dip into fondue. (If fondue becomes too thick, stir in a small amount of half-and-half.)

1 Serving (¼ cup fondue and 6 dippers each): Calories 360 (Calories from Fat 180); Total Fat 20g (Saturated Fat 11g); Cholesterol 35mg; Sodium 55mg; Total Carbohydrate 42g (Dietary Fiber 3g); Protein 5g

Dark Chocolate Fondue [20 servings]

Prep Time: **25 Minutes**   Start to Finish: **25 Minutes**

8 oz bittersweet baking chocolate, chopped

8 oz semisweet baking chocolate, chopped

1 pint (2 cups) whipping cream

1 tablespoon vanilla

1 package (10.75 oz) frozen pound cake, cut into 1-inch cubes

40 small fresh strawberries

40 apple slices

Kiwifruit, cut up, if desired

1   In 2-quart heavy saucepan, heat both chocolates and the whipping cream over low heat, stirring frequently, until cream is hot and chocolate is melted. Stir with whisk until smooth. Stir in vanilla. Pour into fondue pot. Keep warm with fuel canister on low heat.

2   Arrange cake and fruit dippers on platter. Set fondue pot in center of platter.

1 Serving (2½ tablespoons fondue, 1 cake piece, 2 strawberries and 2 apple slices each): Calories 290 (Calories from Fat 190); Total Fat 21g (Saturated Fat 12g); Cholesterol 45mg; Sodium 25mg; Total Carbohydrate 22g (Dietary Fiber 3g); Protein 4g

Instead of the vanilla, try 1 tablespoon of orange-, cherry-, almond- or coffee-flavored liqueur.

Banana chunks, orange or tangerine segments, marshmallows and coconut macaroon cookies also make tasty dippers for this rich fondue.

Chocolate Mousse { 8 servings }

Prep Time: **30 Minutes**   Start to Finish: **2 Hours 40 Minutes**

MOUSSE

4 egg yolks

¼ cup sugar

2½ cups whipping cream

8 oz semisweet baking
chocolate, chopped

CHOCOLATE PIPING

½ cup semisweet chocolate
chips

½ teaspoon shortening

1 In small bowl, beat egg yolks with electric mixer on high
speed about 3 minutes or until thickened and lemon colored.
Gradually beat in sugar.

2 In 2-quart saucepan, heat 1 cup of the whipping cream over
medium heat just until hot. Gradually stir at least half of the hot
cream into egg yolk mixture, then stir egg mixture back into hot
cream in saucepan. Cook over low heat about 5 minutes, stirring
constantly, until mixture thickens (do not boil).

3 Stir in baking chocolate until melted. Cover; refrigerate about 2
hours, stirring occasionally, just until chilled.

4 In chilled medium bowl, beat remaining 1½ cups whipping
cream on high speed until stiff peaks form. Fold chocolate
mixture into whipped cream.

5 In 1-cup microwaveable measuring cup, microwave chocolate
chips and shortening uncovered on Medium 30 seconds. Stir;
microwave in 10-second increments, stirring after each, until
melted and smooth. Place in small resealable food-storage plastic
bag; seal bag. Cut off tiny corner of bag. Squeeze bag to pipe
designs or swirls inside parfait glasses. Refrigerate 10 minutes to
set chocolate.

6 Spoon mousse into glasses. Refrigerate until serving. Store
covered in refrigerator.

1 Serving: Calories 490 (Calories from Fat 330); Total Fat 37g (Saturated Fat 22g); Cholesterol
185mg; Sodium 35mg; Total Carbohydrate 33g (Dietary Fiber 2g); Protein 5g

The cream will whip up faster if you chill the bowl and beaters in the freezer for about 15 minutes before whipping.

metric conversion guide

volume

U.S. Units	Canadian Metric	Australian Metric
¼ teaspoon	1 mL	1 ml
½ teaspoon	2 mL	2 ml
1 teaspoon	5 mL	5 ml
1 tablespoon	15 mL	20 ml
¼ cup	50 mL	60 ml
⅓ cup	75 mL	80 ml
½ cup	125 mL	125 ml
⅔ cup	150 mL	170 ml
¾ cup	175 mL	190 ml
1 cup	250 mL	250 ml
1 quart	1 liter	1 liter
1½ quarts	1.5 liters	1.5 liters
2 quarts	2 liters	2 liters
2½ quarts	2.5 liters	2.5 liters
3 quarts	3 liters	3 liters
4 quarts	4 liters	4 liters

weight

U.S. Units	Canadian Metric	Australian Metric
1 ounce	30 grams	30 grams
2 ounces	55 grams	60 grams
3 ounces	85 grams	90 grams
4 ounces (¼ pound)	115 grams	125 grams
8 ounces (½ pound)	225 grams	225 grams
16 ounces (1 pound)	455 grams	500 grams
1 pound	455 grams	0.5 kilogram

NOTE: The recipes in this cookbook have not been developed or tested using metric measures. When converting recipes to metric, some variations in quality may be noted.

measurements

Inches	Centimeters
1	2.5
2	5.0
3	7.5
4	10.0
5	12.5
6	15.0
7	17.5
8	20.5
9	23.0
10	25.5
11	28.0
12	30.5
13	33.0

temperatures

Fahrenheit	Celsius
32°	0°
212°	100°
250°	120°
275°	140°
300°	150°
325°	160°
350°	180°
375°	190°
400°	200°
425°	220°
450°	230°
475°	240°
500°	260°

Recipe Index

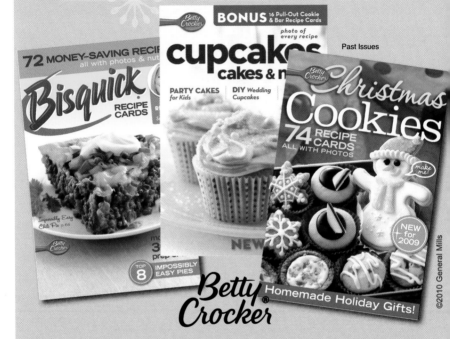